Department of
the Environment

Ancient Monuments and
Historic Buildings

DOVER CASTLE

R Allen Brown MA, D Phil, FSA

Her Majesty's
Stationery Office

Right: View of the castle from the north, 1735

Few if any fortified sites in England are more impressive than Dover Castle, and few even in Wales, the land of castles. Once entered in, the visitor is likely to be absorbed by and lost among the widespread component parts of the great fortress, and is strongly urged to obtain, either on arrival or on departure, a general view of the castle's total grandeur – from the town below, where the castle seems to occupy the entire skyline, or from the Deal Road beyond the site to the north-east, or from the high ground immediately north. Reference to the plan and aerial photograph printed in this guide will also help, while there is a fine and large-scale aerial photograph upon the wall of the restaurant within the inner bailey.

At Dover there is something for everybody. The lofty site on Castle Hill, made strong by nature as well as by man, commands the adjacent harbour which opens on the shortest crossing to the Continent; so it has been occupied and usually fortified in almost every period of English history. The original earthworks, which still define the shape and extent of the medieval castle upon them, first formed an Iron Age fortress. Within this the Romans placed their *pharos* or lighthouse, which survives adjacent to the church of St Mary-in-Castro. In the later Anglo-Saxon period, it seems that the already ancient earthworks were re-used and occupied to make of them a *borough* or fortified township, to which the same church, Anglo-Saxon in date though much restored, still stands as witness. Here, too, the Normans came immediately after Hastings in 1066 to plant their castle within the *borough*. Maintained in good order throughout the Middle Ages, the castle received some Tudor outworks, and figured in the seventeenth-century Civil War between King and Parliament. In the period of the Napoleonic Wars when invasion seemed to threaten once again from France, it was refurbished and extensively adapted to more modern warfare – with unhappy results upon the medieval architecture, almost all the towers being cut down in height to make gun platforms. Dover remained occupied by the Army until as recently as 1958, and only in 1963 was the whole monument turned over to the custody of what is now the Department of the Environment. Meanwhile, in the dark days of 1940–41, the skies above the ancient castle were filled with historic fighting of another kind. In the thirteenth century Matthew Paris called Dover "the key of England"; and so it has remained down to our own times.

Above: View from the north, showing St John's Tower, the blocked North Gateway and Constable's Gate

The history of the present medieval castle, as opposed to the pre-

existing Saxon and Iron Age earthworks whose site it occupies, begins with the Norman Conquest. It used to be thought that Dover might belong to a small, select group of English pre-Conquest castles; but it now seems clear that references to Dover "castle" in 1051 and 1064 are to a fortified township upon the cliff, and it was this which Duke William of Normandy was anxious to acquire both as a surety and as an advance base for his succession to the English throne promised him by Edward the Confessor. Probably it was the attempted occupation of Dover on the duke's behalf by his ally Count Eustace of Boulogne in 1051 that occasioned the rebellion of Earl Godwin of Wessex; and certainly in 1064, when Earl Harold took his famous oath to William upon the relics at Bayeux, he was made to swear not only that he would support the duke's claim to be Edward the Confessor's heir but also that he would make over Dover to him.

Immediately after their great victory at Hastings in 1066, before advancing upon London, the Normans made for Dover, which was surrendered to them, and there the Norman chronicler, William of Poitiers, tells us William the Conqueror spent eight days in adding those fortifications it lacked. There is little doubt that this addition was the first castle of Dover, made by cutting off, by ditch and bank and

palisade, a section of the larger enclosure of Saxon borough and Iron Age earthworks.

The castle was soon to prove its worth and strength, for in 1067, while William, now king, was celebrating his English victory in Normandy, it was attacked by the men of Kent in league with Count Eustace of Boulogne. The attack was meant to be by surprise, but though the two custodians to whom the new fortress had been entrusted – the king's half-brother, Bishop Odo of Bayeux, and Hugh de Montfort – were both away on other military business together with many of their knights, the garrison remaining easily beat off their assailants with heavy losses and in total confusion.

Of this, the first and Norman castle of Dover, nothing is now visible, though archaeological research has recently revealed some trace of it in the form of a ditch and bank close by the south side of St Mary's church and beneath the present thirteenth-century earthworks there. The earliest work the visitor can see, and see in prodigious quantities, is that of Henry II, who undertook the rebuilding of the castle in stone,

Below: The Bayeux Tapestry. Earl Harold taking the Oath before William the Conqueror when Harold swore that he would support William's claim to the English throne and that he would make over the Anglo-Saxon borough of Dover to him

principally in the 1180s. The cost of some £7000 was enormous by the standards of the age and far exceeds the known cost of any other English castle of the period. As indication of the value of money then, it may be noted that the king's chief architect at Dover, Master Maurice the Mason, or Engineer, received at first 8d and later 1s a day as his wages. In return for this expenditure of money, and also labour, Henry had much to show. His works comprised the great rectangular tower keep, the centre and donjon of the castle, majestic, complex and immensely strong (which will be separately described below), together with the walls, towers and gateways of the inner bailey which surrounds it, with barbicans or outworks to north and south and further works connecting the southern barbican with the former Penchester Tower on the outer curtain to the east. In addition, a long section of the outer curtain of the castle to north and east is also Henry's work, at least from a point just beyond the (later) Fitzwilliam Gate southwards to Penchester, and possibly continuing south again to the cliff. Lastly, a ditch and rampart, predecessors of the present

Above: Treasurer's Tower and Godsfoe Tower

Above Right: Constable's Gate

much larger thirteenth-century ones, about the church of St Mary, may date from his time or may be earlier.

The great keep is one of the finest of its kind. The walls of the inner bailey and the outer curtain systematically incorporate mural towers which by projecting out in front enable the exposed outer face of the walls to be defended by lateral covering fire. The polygonal Avranches Tower with its double tier of loops for the cross-bow is particularly formidable. These towers also divide the walls into separate, sealed-off sections, and by their original height (before they were cut down) enabled superior fire power to be directed down upon any assailants who gained the top of the walls by escalade or ladder. The gateways of the inner bailey, King's Gate and Palace Gate, are also noteworthy. Each was originally defended by a walled barbican or outwork of which only the north barbican by King's Gate survives. The gateways themselves are formed by bringing together a pair of mural towers one on either side of the entrance passage; this arrangement is the origin of the design of nearly all the great gatehouses of later English medieval castles. Dover also provides the earliest known example in England or on the Continent of concentric fortification, that is, one line within another, such as was perfected by Edward I a century later in Wales at Harlech and Beaumaris,

and is sometimes attributed to him as though he were its inventor.

Richard I spent a further £600 in 1189–90 to finish off his father's work. In the reign of John, after the loss of Normandy, there was serious danger of a French invasion; therefore, as a measure of coastal defence, a sum which certainly exceeds £1000 was spent upon Dover between 1205 and 1214. Much was evidently disbursed upon the completion of the outer curtain about the north end of the castle, beginning where Henry II had left off in the area of the present Fitz-william Gate (which then did not exist) and continuing round and

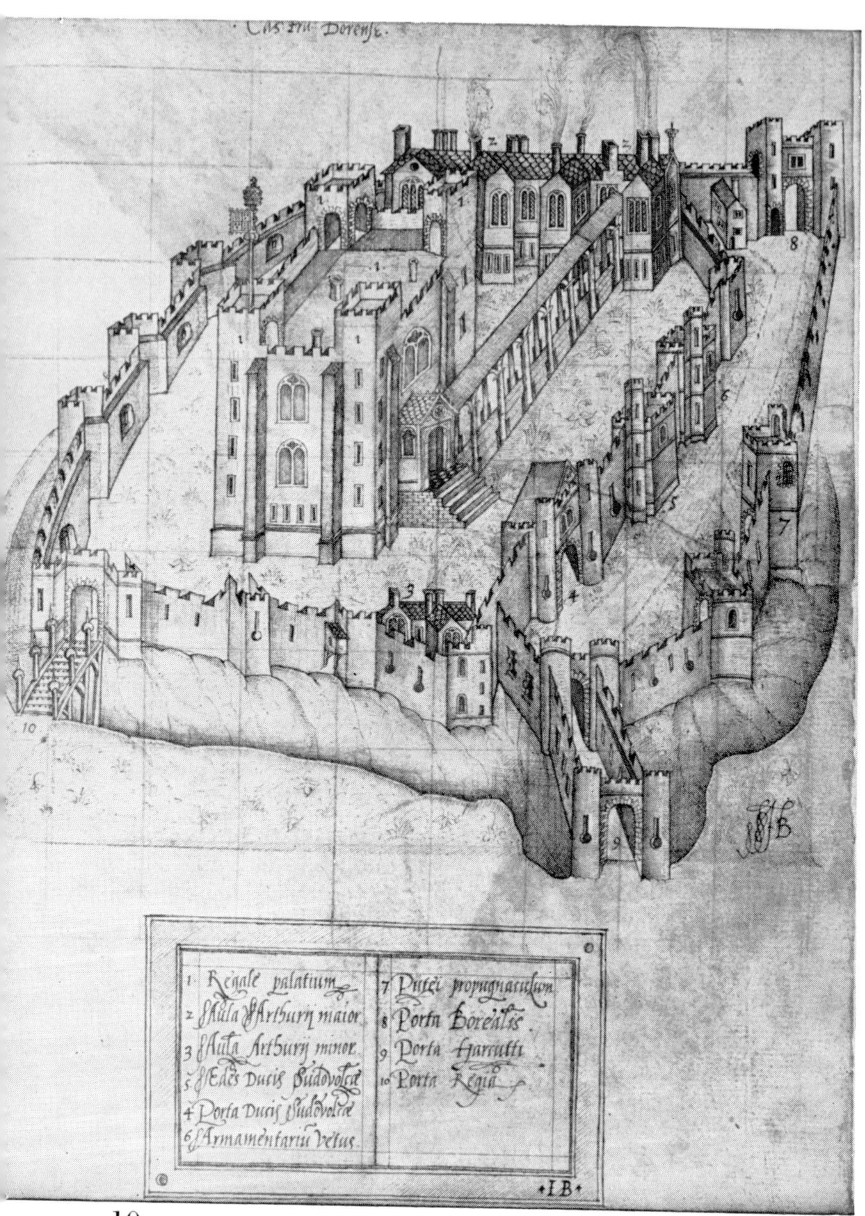
Castrum Dorense
1 Regale palatium
2 Aula Arthurij maior
3 Aula Arthurij minor
5 Edes Ducis Sudovolcie
4 Porta Ducis Sudovolcie
6 Armamentariu Vetus
7 Putei propugnaculum
8 Porta Borealis
9 Porta Harcutti
10 Porta Regia
IB

down to the western tower of Peverell's Gate. With the exception of Godsfoe Tower and the Treasurer's Tower, the mural towers of this section are D-shaped with a rounded projection towards the field, and are thus distinguishable from the rectangular towers of Henry II. King John did not build the splendid Constable's Gate which is now the main outer gateway of the castle in the north-west; that came later. John's outer gate was at the northern apex of the castle, where the Norfolk Towers now stand, in line with King's Gate of the inner bailey, and consisting of two great D-shaped towers, one on either side of the entrance passage. It seems clear that John also raised a lesser wall across the castle, from Peverell's Tower to Colton's Gate which he also built (the former was altered in the later thirteenth century and the latter in the fifteenth), and so round the church on the forward slope of the twelfth-century rampart to rejoin the outer curtain on the eastern side by the vanished towers of Ashford and Godwin.

This reign ended with civil war, when Dover Castle withstood – but only just – the greatest siege of its history. Held for King John by Hubert de Burgh, Chief Justiciar of England, it was attacked in 1216 by Prince Louis, son of the King of France, whom those barons in opposition to the king had invited to England to take the throne. Louis and his knights concentrated their efforts against John's new outer gate. First they took the barbican or outwork which defended it, and then they dug a mine or underground shaft down beneath the gate itself, and were so successful that they brought down the eastern of its two towers. Hubert and his garrison were able to plug the breach with timber baulks and the strength of their own right arms, and continued to hold out until the death of John and the succession of his infant son Henry III brought about the end of the war. But a weakness in the castle's defences had been revealed. The next reign was to make it good.

Between 1217 and 1256, some £7500 was spent upon Dover Castle, or as much again as it had cost Henry II to begin but not complete it. The first task was to fill the breach that Prince Louis' miners had made and to make impossible any repetition of their machinations. As a result the defensive arrangements of the castle towards the north were transformed and greatly strengthened. First the damaged twin-towered gateway of King John was both repaired

Left: View of the Keep and Inner Bailey from the west by Bereblock (sixteenth century)

We are indebted to the College of Arms for permission to reproduce this drawing from their Philpot Collection, MS.P.b.47

and closed. The eastern tower which had been undermined was rebuilt solid and joined to its undamaged western fellow by another solid tower, 'beaked' or pointed towards the field, like the prow of a ship and in what was then the latest military fashion, thus blocking for ever the entrance passage of the former gate, and forming the proud trinity of the Norfolk Towers. Next, the area of the former barbican in front of John's gate, and the high ground beyond, were denied to any future enemy by the construction of a great outwork or spur (still there but altered and cased in brick in the Napoleonic period) and of the cylindrical St John's Tower in

the ditch between this spur and the castle. Castle, tower and spur were then joined by subterranean passage-ways, originals of the present underground works. The Fitzwilliam Towers, again 'beaked', were built into the outer curtain on the north-east, to form a postern gate or sally-port, with a covered passage-way across the ditch and through the bank beyond, whence sorties could be launched towards the vital northern sector. In this way, and at vast expense, a notable exercise in locking the stable door after the horse has been stolen was completed. Finally, the splendid Constable's Gate in the north-west sector of the castle is known

Above: The embarkation of Henry VIII for

to have been under construction in 1221 and was probably completed by 1227.

Much of the remainder of Henry III's great expenditure on Dover went upon the completion of the outer curtain walls and towers, certainly on the west from Peverell's Gate to the cliff, and possibly on the east from Ashford Tower southwards. He caused to be re-dug on a much greater scale the horseshoe rampart about the church of St Mary, crowned his rampart with a wall in 1256, and repaired the

ield of Cloth of Gold. Dover, May 1520

church itself. Paying attention to the residential accommodation within the castle, he built new ranges of domestic buildings within the inner bailey to replace those of John and Henry II east of the keep and including hall, chambers, chapel and kitchen. Much of this is still there though mutilated and heavily disguised by conversion into eighteenth-century barrack blocks.

Thus by about 1256 the medieval castle of Dover attained its maximum strength and size, in appearance much as it is today, and had come to occupy the whole site of the earlier Anglo-Saxon borough and Iron Age fortress. The only further major work to be carried out during the Middle Ages was that commissioned by Edward IV (1461–1483), who built the present Fulbert of Dover's Tower and Treasurer's Tower on the western outer curtain, and who modernised the keep to make its appearance conform more closely to the architectural fashion of his age. Though some are restored, most of the window openings outside, and most of the doorways together with the fire-places inside, are the result of his extensive alterations; some of the last still bear his Yorkist badge of the rose *en soleil*.

Henry VIII's wars with France and the possibility of a French invasion led to the enlargement and further defence of Dover harbour; as part of this operation the Tudor Bulwark was added to the southern extremity of the castle, and the Moat's Bulwark (much altered later) was constructed below the castle cliff. At the outbreak of the seventeenth-century Civil War the castle was regarded as of sufficient importance for a small but determined party of men from the town to seize it by surprise, and it was thereafter held for Parliament in spite of Royalist attempts to recapture it – which may account for the absence of any of that Parliamentary "slighting" or demolition which ruined so many good castles. Neglect then set in for a century until the threatening ruination was either averted or accelerated – according to one's point of view – by successive adaptations of the ancient castle to meet the demands of new warfare from the mid-eighteenth century onwards and especially in the Napoleonic period. Towers have been cut down and walls earthed up; the southern barbican has gone, likewise the outer curtain on the east side from Penchester Tower to the sea; Hubert de Burgh's spur has become a brick-encased redoubt, there are barracks in the inner bailey, and even the upper and grander storey of the keep, where once the kings of England stayed, has been mutilated by ugly "bomb-proof arches". Dover Castle became merely one of a series of forts and fortifications about and above the harbour, from the Western Heights on the other side, through Fort Burgoyne on the north, to the Shoulder of Mutton Battery south-east of the castle.

Dover's scale is so vast, and there is so much to see, that the visitor may well be at a loss to know where to begin. Entrance is now usually made through Canons Gate, built in the 1790s at the south end of the western outer curtain, and thence one proceeds north, past Queen Elizabeth's Pocket Pistol. Though the ornamental carriage on which it is mounted dates only from 1827, this splendid gun, 24ft long, was made at Utrecht in 1544 and given to Henry VIII by the Emperor

Right: The Keep

The Avranches Tower

Charles V. It has near the breech an inscription which may be translated:

Breaker my name of rampart and wall
Over hill and dale I throw my ball.

Soon after this the visitor passes through Peverell's Gate and moves towards Henry II's inner bailey. Hereabouts, the bulk of the Constable's Gate appears on the left. From the time when it was built in the 1220s this gatehouse has been the residence of the constable of the castle or (as now) his deputy. The back of the tower, that is, inside the castle and facing the visitor, was much restored in 1882; outside, the elegant Georgian sash windows are, of course, alterations, as are the pretty little balcony and the ugly brick casemates between the tall piers of the medieval bridge.

The roadway leading off outside from Constable's Gate affords a splendid view of castle ditch and bank, the latter bearing the north-west section of the outer curtain, mostly built by King John, running through Treasurer's, Godsfoe and Crevecoeur Towers, and curving round to the three Norfolk Towers, King John's former gateway at the northern apex, with St John's Tower standing guard out in front. From this landward side the castle was most vulnerable at least until all the belated thirteenth-century precautions were taken after the siege of 1216, and hereabout Prince Louis must have stood, or sat his horse, to decide upon his method of attack. Beyond all this potent array of thirteenth-century military architecture, if the visitor cares to stroll further, are the twin beaked towers of Fitzwilliam Gate, with its caponier or covered passage-way across the ditch, and beyond this again the projecting rectangular towers of Henry II's stretch of the outer curtain, terminating in his polygonal Avranches Tower.

Inside the castle, Henry II's inner bailey and, above all, his great keep must certainly be visited. The best view of the wall of the inner bailey, with its projecting rectangular mural towers, is obtained from the area of Constable's Gate, and the interior of one tower can be seen within the restaurant. The inner bailey itself can be entered either through King's Gate to the north or through Palace Gate to the south. The former retains its protecting barbican or outwork while the latter does not. Along the inside of the bailey walls, there once stood a complex of medieval domestic apartments. The present buildings, of 1745, incorporate some of their walls, preserve much of their plan and, on the east, a little detail of Henry III's time.

The dominating feature of the inner bailey is the great rectangular keep, whose overwhelming bulk occupies the centre of it. Built at a cost of anything up to £4000 (more than enough at that time to build an entire castle), it rises from its splayed-out base or plinth to a height of 95ft, and measures 98 by 96ft in area, without counting the fore-building which projects from it on two sides to cover the entrance. Its walls, of Kentish ragstone with dressings of finer stone from Caen in Normandy, are of immense thickness, varying from 21ft at the base to 17ft, without counting either the plinth or the buttresses in the centre of each face and at the corners (where they form corner turrets rising above the level of the roof). The whole building is given even greater solidity by an internal cross wall which divides it into two roughly equal halves within, and helps to carry the weight of the roof. This great tower was designed with a dual purpose: to be the ultimate stronghold which could be held even if the rest of the castle fell, and to contain some of the best residential accommodation. King Henry's engineers and masons combined the two functions of fighting and living within a confined space at least as ingeniously as the designers of a modern submarine.

Left: Newel stairs in the north-east tower of the Keep

Right: Upper Chapel in the Keep

Above a basement used mainly for storage and cooking are two residential floors, each level being connected by two wide and splendid stairways, one in the north-east angle and one in the south-west, extending from basement to roof. Each floor was designed as a self-contained suite of apartments for living on the grand medieval scale. The plan of each is similar, comprising two very large rooms, which doubtless served as Great Hall and Great Chamber respectively, one on either side of the central cross wall which divides them, with lesser chambers opening off them and contrived within the thickness of the walls or within the towers of the adjacent forebuilding. Originally the second residential floor was much the grander, and was doubtless intended for the king himself or any other important visitor of the first rank. Often with tower residences of the Middle Ages, the more elevated you were the higher you lived. Thus in the keep at Dover the two main apartments of the second floor were much loftier than their counterparts beneath, rising in fact through two stages with a mural gallery about them to provide more light and spaciousness;

there was more architectural decoration (for example, on the window openings), while the chapel is more elaborate than the one beneath, and can be reached direct from the living rooms without crossing the forebuilding. The principal entrance to the keep is also at this second-

The Roman Pharos

floor level, reached through the forebuilding which characteristically is one of the most impressive in all England, and was meant to be. It consists basically of three flights of steps ascending round two sides of the keep through three turrets or lesser towers which project from the main block of the building. Each flight of steps was originally open to the sky, and could thus be defended by covering fire from the top of the tower above it.

The keep is entered, now as in the beginning, through the forebuilding. Near the foot of the first flight of steps there is an entrance straight into the basement – an unusual and rather risky feature, but now thought to be a later alteration. It was in any case well defended, by the first forebuilding tower and also originally by three doors within its entrance passage, one behind the other and each with a drawbar. At the top of this first flight of steps, the visitor enters the lower vestibule of the forebuilding, elegantly arcaded on the southern side, with a porter's lodge on the right behind him and the beautiful lower chapel on the right in front. From the lower vestibule one turns sharp left to ascend two further flights of steps, with a drawbridge pit between them (now crossed by modern steps and bridge) at the approach to the second and centre turret of the forebuilding. At the foot of the first stairway there is, on the left, a fifteenth-century doorway now opening into the custodian's office but formerly leading into the first-floor apartments of the keep. At the top of the second there is an upper entrance vestibule, with a guardroom in front of one and, on one's left, the great doorway into the second floor of the keep, carved and moulded as befits the entrance of the state apartments.

Through this doorway, on the left of the entrance passage (which itself reveals the thickness of the walls at this level) is the well chamber. The well head was brought up to this level to serve the principal, upper floor, and thus plummets down sheer through the whole structure of the keep and deep into the natural chalk below. Left of the well head there is a recessed stone sink in which can still be seen the mouths of two leaden pipes intended to convey water to other parts of the keep. The well is in itself an impressive engineering feat, while the refinement of a piped water supply in a late twelfth-century building may perhaps surprise the modern visitor.

At the end of the entrance passage, steps lead down into the second-floor apartments. Here are two very large rooms, interconnected both by a doorway at the northern end of the cross wall and by a passage-way and chamber entered from the stepped-up window embrasures at their southern ends. Though they retain their great window embrasures, their former grandeur has been ruined by brick vaults inserted in 1800. The walls of both rooms are marked with *graffiti* of French prisoners of war. The first room entered shows near its south-east corner the curious feature of an archway, 5ft above the floor and set in modern brick, opening into a small mural chamber whose use is unknown. The other room has its fifteenth-century fireplace unaltered, though restored, with Edward IV's Yorkist badges of the rose *en soleil*. Probably it served as the Great Chamber. To the right of its west window, a doorway leads into what was no doubt intended as the bedroom of the king.

The chapel of this second floor is reached through the mural chambers and passages leading off from the southern window embrasures of the two great rooms. At the end of a remarkably narrow passage one finds on the right a sacristy, and on the left first an ante-chapel and then the chapel proper. The sacristy has low stone benches round three sides; sacristy, ante-chapel and chapel alike are finely built and richly decorated with wall arcades, arches with chevron ornament, carved capitals, and groined vaults; and all have the attraction of being still in use.

The first floor of the keep can be reached from the upper floor by either of the two great spiral stairways. Its residential accommodation is laid out in almost exactly the same way as that of the main floor, though its chapel could be reached only by passing through what is now the custodian's office and crossing the lower vestibule of the forebuilding. There are, however, some differences and particular features. Each of the two large main apartments has its fifteenth-century fireplace more or less intact with the Yorkist badges, and this time they are each in the exact centre of the cross wall. The eastern apartment, moreover, which now contains a fine scale model of the battlefield of Waterloo (made in the 1830s by Captain William Siborne), was framed in heavy timbers on its eastern and western sides in the thirteenth century (presumably to reinforce the floor above).

The basement of the keep is naturally somewhat gloomy. As on the residential floors, the basic plan is of two main central rooms with mural chambers or rooms opening off. The two main rooms are smaller than those upstairs because of the huge thickness of the walls at this ground level, but more room is obtained for storage and moving stores by piercing the cross wall with three large archways. The direct entrance, already described, from the forebuilding steps into the basement shows traces of its original closure by three doors and three drawbars. One long and narrow mural chamber, which contains a great oven, is reached by a passage from the north-east stairway.

The energetic visitor is likely to want to climb up one of the spiral stairways to the roof, with its traces of mountings of the heavy guns of the post-medieval period, and its panoramic views of castle, town and harbour, the countryside and sea beyond, and, on a clear day, the coast of France. He may also explore the mural gallery which opens off the spiral stairways and surrounds the upper residential floor; this is not quite continuous, but is blocked on the north by a small chamber with a privy.

Down below there are other parts of the castle still to be visited. The underground works at the north end are a popular attraction. Entrance to them is beneath the ruined causeway leading from the Norfolk Towers to the northern barbican and entrance of the inner bailey. They were constructed in the early thirteenth century and altered in Napoleonic times, the later period being easily recognized by its brickwork. On the way down, the medieval tunnel, cut through the natural chalk, is crossed diagonally by a smaller, rough-hewn gallery which may be a mining tunnel of Prince Louis' sappers in 1216, while a little further on an iron grating beneath one's feet shows

The Fitzwilliam Gate

another tunnel. Next one enters St John's Tower at first-floor level but on a modern floor. This tower, also built in the early thirteenth century, stands in the middle of the castle ditch, and originally consisted of a basement and three upper storeys. The underground works continue towards the spur, through defences part medieval and part Napoleonic. Originally they divided into three branching passageways each leading out to sortie points; now only the left-hand passage goes on to reach two Napoleonic guardrooms. The entrance to these from outside is defended by a most ingenious system of remote-controlled doors arranged to form a deadly booby trap for any hostile intruder.

South of the keep and modern car park, within the great horseshoe-shaped earthwork of Henry III, stand the two oldest buildings in Dover Castle, the Roman *pharos* or lighthouse and the church of St Mary-in-Castro. The *pharos*, which once had a fellow on the opposite Western Heights, was built probably in the first century AD. In shape octagonal outside, rectangular within, it rose to a height of about 80ft through eight stages or storeys each slightly set back from the one beneath to give the whole a stepped or telescopic appearance. It is now much weathered and refaced and has only five stages left, the lowest four being Roman. The *pharos* became the bell-tower of the adjacent church of St Mary, which was built in the late tenth or early eleventh century, probably to serve the Anglo-Saxon borough or fortified township. As a late Saxon church, cruciform in shape, the building is of much interest, but unfortunately it was horribly over-restored in the late nineteenth century. It is possible to detect re-used Roman brick throughout, and, in the nave, two double-splayed windows, and the south door from the late Saxon period.

Key to facing Plan

1 Tudor Bulwark and Canons Gate
2 Fulbert of Dover's Tower
3 Peverell's Tower and Gate
4 Queen Mary's Tower
5 Constable's Tower and Gate
6 Treasurer's Tower
7 Godsfoe Tower
8 Crevecoeur Tower
9 Norfolk Towers
10 St John's Tower
11 Underground passages
12 Fitzwilliam Gate
13 Avranches Tower
14 Penchester Tower
15 North Barbican
16 King's Gate
17 Inner Bailey
18 Keep
19 Palace Gate
20 Colton Gate
21 Pharos
22 Church of St Mary-in-Castro

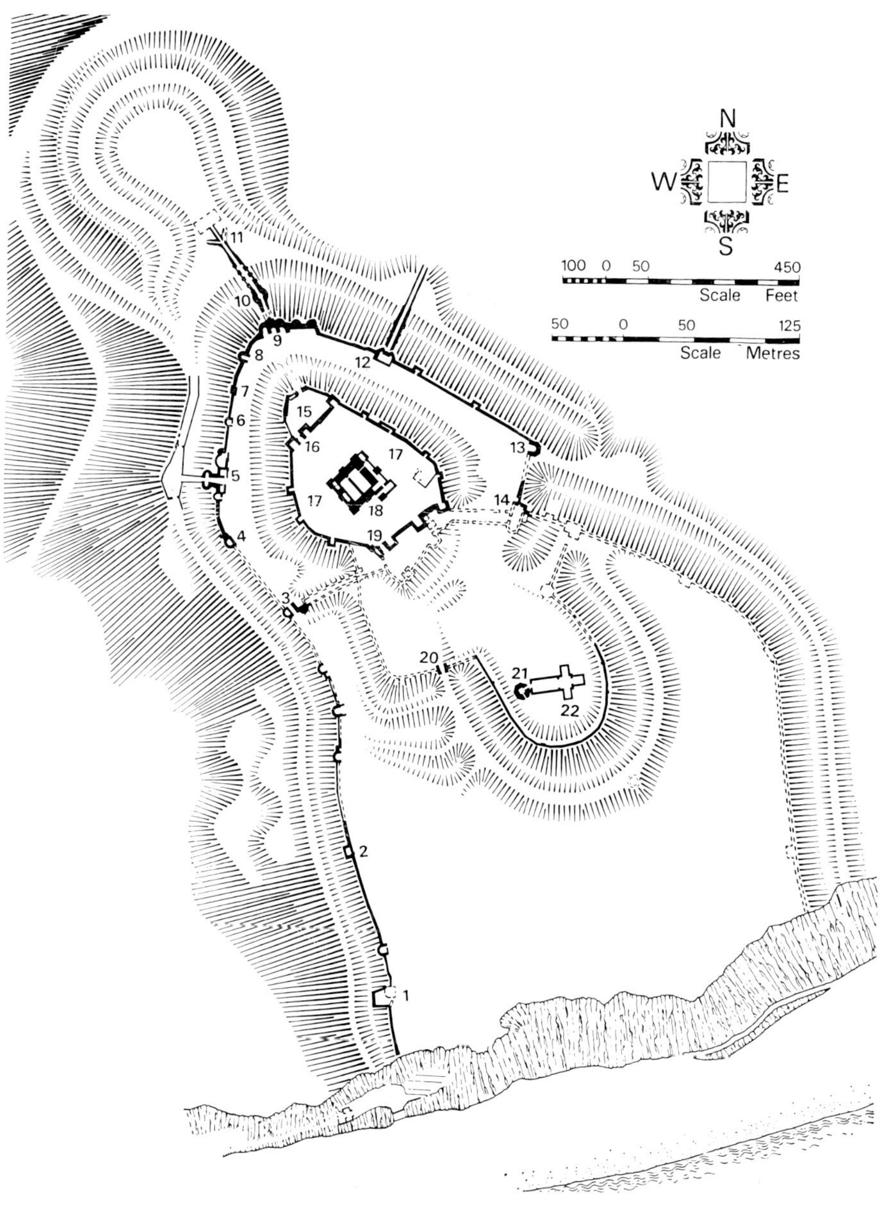
N
W
E
S
100 0 50 450
Scale Feet
50 0 50 125
Scale Metres
1
2
3
4
5
6
7
8
9
10
11
12
13
14
15
16
17
17
18
19
20
21
22

Some notable Constables of Dover Castle

1066–1084	Odo, Bishop of Bayeux and Earl of Kent
1202–1232	Hubert de Burgh, Earl of Kent
1265–1298	Sir Stephen de Pencestre
1409–1413	Henry, Prince of Wales (afterwards King Henry V)
1415–1447	Humphrey, Duke of Gloucester
1493–1505	Henry, Duke of York (afterwards King Henry VIII)
1660–1669	James, Duke of York (afterwards King James II)
1792–1805	William Pitt
1828–1852	The Duke of Wellington
1860–1865	Lord Palmerston
1905–1907	George, Prince of Wales (afterwards King George V)
1941–1965	Sir Winston Churchill

How to get there

There is a good train service from London via Folkestone or Canterbury to Dover Priory Station. Dover Castle stands conspicuously on the hill to the east of the town. Frequent buses on Service 80 start from Pencester Road, in the centre of Dover, and pass up Castle Hill Road near Constable's Gate entrance to the Castle.

SEASON TICKETS, valid for a year from the date of issue, admit their holders to all ancient monuments and historic buildings in the care of the State. Tickets can be purchased at many monuments, at HMSO bookshops and from the Department of the Environment (AMHB/P), 25 Savile Row, London W1X 2BT, which will supply full information on request.

Printed in England for Her Majesty's Stationery Office by Swindon Press Ltd., Swindon.
(012E) Dd 496991 K340 12/76 Gp 469